PLAY

By Joanna Brundle

A Look at Life Around the World

BookLife
PUBLISHING

©2018
Book Life
King's Lynn
Norfolk PE30 4LS

ISBN: 978-1-78637-471-4

All rights reserved
Printed in Malaysia

Written by:
Joanna Brundle

Edited by:
Kirsty Holmes

Designed by:
Jasmine Pointer

A catalogue record for this book
is available from the British Library.

All facts, statistics, web addresses
and URLs in this book were verified
as valid and accurate at time of
writing. No responsibility for any
changes to external websites or
references can be accepted by
either the author or publisher.

CONTENTS

Words that look like <u>this</u> can be found in the glossary on page 23.

ALL KINDS OF GAMES AND TOYS

Children everywhere love to play, outside and inside, alone and together. Some games are played quietly while others are lively and noisy. Some need special equipment. Others just need your imagination. Playing is fun, but it also teaches you new skills, like following rules and sharing.

These children are playing video games.

Let's go on a trip around the world to find out how children just like you enjoy their playtime. As you read, think about your favourite games and toys. What do you like about them and why are they special to you and your friends?

HOPPING AND JUMPING GAMES

Hopscotch is played all around the world. Players draw a <u>grid</u> with numbers and hop their way along, throwing a pebble as they go. In France, children call this game 'escargot', meaning 'snail'. The grid is drawn in a spiral shape, like a snail's shell.

In Majorca, Spanish hopscotch is called 'spider'. The grid is the shape of a spider's web and neither the pebble nor your foot can touch a number or line.

These girls in Vietnam are having fun skipping. Skipping games are played all over the world.

Maklot is a jumping game played in Israel. Three sticks are placed on the ground. Players take it in turns to jump over the sticks without touching them and keeping both feet together. If they touch the sticks or separate their feet, they are out. Each round, the sticks are moved farther apart.

HAND GAMES JAN KEN PON

Jan Ken Pon, which means Rock, Paper, Scissors, is a game played in Japan. The two players stand facing one another. At the signal, players make one of these signs with their hand. The rock beats the scissors. The scissors beat the paper. The paper beats the rock. The best of five games wins.

Children play different <u>versions</u> of this game all over the world.

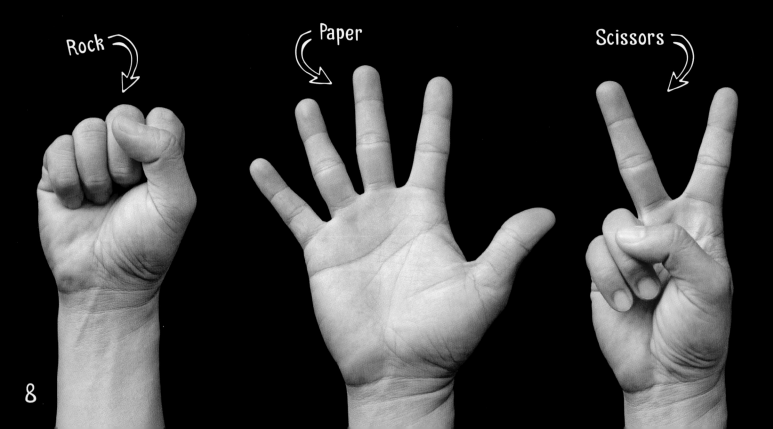

Rock

Paper

Scissors

These children are playing 'Miss Mary Mack', another popular game in the USA.

Clapping games are played all around the world. Children clap to a <u>rhythm</u> and sing or chant a <u>rhyme</u> as they clap. In the USA, children play a clapping game for four people, called Rockin' Robin. Players stand in circle and clap across and to the players at each side, while bouncing their knees.

BOARD GAMES

The board game of Go was invented in China 2,500 years ago. It is very popular throughout Asia. Two players use either black or white pieces called stones and try to cover more of the board than the other player. In Japan, Go is called 'Igo' and in Korea it is known as 'Baduk'.

Players have to plan ahead and <u>concentrate</u> hard to win.

Go has even been played by astronauts in space.

Mancala is an ancient board game, played in Asia and Africa.
It is played using pieces called seeds and a board with small pits.
The winner is the person with the most amount of seeds at the end
of the game. The 'seeds' are usually beans, stones or shells.

Mancala boards can be beautifully decorated.

These children in Ethiopia have dug small holes in the ground to make their board.

CHASING AND CATCHING GAMES

Blind Man's Bluff, in which the catcher wears a blindfold, is played all over Europe.

Tag is a chasing and catching game. In the USA, children also play 'Fox and Geese'. Players draw a large circle on the ground with lines criss-crossing through the middle. The person chosen to be the fox tries to catch the others (the geese). A goose who is caught becomes the next fox. Everyone has to stay on the lines.

Children in China play 'Catch the Dragon's Tail'. Players form a line and place their hands on the shoulders of the person in front. The first person is the dragon's head and has to catch the person at the other end, who is the tail. The line must not break.

This game is often played during celebrations for Chinese New Year.

The dragon is a <u>symbol</u> of good luck in China.

GAMES OF SKILL AND STRENGTH

The balero is a small, traditional toy that is popular with children all over America and Asia. It has a cup or ball and a stick with a narrow end. These are attached to opposite ends of a piece of string. Players try to catch the cup or ball on the narrow end of the stick.

The fiorete is a special move from Bolivia in which the cup or ball is swung round in circles before being caught.

A version of this game called Kendama is played in Japan.

Different versions of Tug-of-War are played all over the world.

In Sudan, children play Haneque. They draw a circle on the ground and divide into two teams. One person from the attacking team tries to enter the circle. The other team tries to push or pull them away. All players have to hop on one leg, holding the other leg with one hand.

HANDMADE TOYS

Children all around the world enjoy tyre swings.

This is a handmade galimoto made by a child.

Some children make their own toys from things they find. A football can be made from paper bags and elastic bands. An old tyre makes a great swing. Across Africa, children make galimotos. These are wheeled toy cars, made from <u>recycled</u> wire and other materials such as sticks and corn stalks.

16

In villages across Nepal, a huge swing known as a linge ping is built once a year. It is part of a religious festival called Dashain. Everyone helps to make the swing using tall <u>bamboo</u> sticks. The sticks are held together with ropes made from jute, which is a type of tough grass.

Everyone waits for their turn and the grown-ups join in the fun too!

DOLLS

The largest Russian doll ever made has 51 pieces. The tallest measures 54 centimetres (cm) and the shortest less than half a centimetre.

Russian dolls, also called matryoshka dolls, are brightly painted sets of dolls that fit inside one another. All the dolls in a set are painted in the same colours and design. Each doll can be pulled apart to show a smaller doll inside.

Children in Guatemala and Mexico tell their worries to worry dolls before they go to sleep. They then place the dolls under their pillow. In the morning, the worry has gone!

Worry Dolls

In the Ukraine, motanka dolls are given to children. The dolls have an <u>embroidered</u> cross instead of a face.

Motanka dolls are believed to keep a child safe.

TEAM GAMES

Cricket is India's most popular game. Children play it in the street, in the park, or practice on a pitch.

Ice hockey is an exciting, fast-moving game that is popular in Canada and Russia. Players wear gloves, helmets and face guards.

Boys and girls everywhere love to play football. It is the world's most popular sport. Some children play for junior teams, while other children play wherever they can, such as in the park or the street. Some of the world's best players, like Neymar, began playing football in the street with their friends.

FUN WITH WATER AND SNOW

In Thailand, people celebrate New Year with the Songkran water festival. Children have great fun soaking everyone with water pistols.

It's hot during Songkran so nobody minds getting wet!

In snowy countries like Canada, Sweden and Norway, children enjoy snowball fights and sliding downhill on sledges and snow tubes. Snow tubes are made from tough plastic so that they don't burst.

Hold on tight!

GLOSSARY

bamboo   a tough, woody plant whose stems can be used for making and building things

concentrate   think very hard about something

embroidered   a raised pattern sewn into fabric

grid   a network of lines

recycled   used again for a different purpose

rhyme   a verse in which two or more lines sound similar, especially the last words of the lines

rhythm   a regular, repeated pattern of sounds, beats or movements

symbol   something you can see that stands for something else that you cannot see, like good luck

versions   different examples of something

INDEX

Photocredits: Abbreviations: l-left, r-right, b-bottom, t-top, c-centre, m-middle.
All images are courtesy of Shutterstock.com. With thanks to Getty Images, Thinkstock Photo and iStockphoto.

Front cover - Robert Kneschke, astudio, Anton_Ivanov. 2 - Stephane Bidouze. 4 - Iakov Filimonov. 5 - wavebreakmedia. 6 - NadyaEugene. 7 – thi. 8 - GOLFX. 9 - Maria Uspenskaya. 10 - Axel Bueckert. 11t - Harismoyo. 11b - Magdalena Paluchowska. 12 - Iakov Filimonov. 13 - ChameleonsEye. 14r - Aurora Angeles. 14l – Jinga. 15 - Robert Kneschke. 16t - Jim David. 16b - Adam Jan Figel. 17 - Nick Fox. 18 - chirajuti. 19t – duckeesue. 19b – Sidhe. 20t - Vitaly Khodyrev. 20b - Sergei Butorin. 21 – lazyllama. 22t - Krieng Meemano. 22b – tammykayphoto.